SPOOKED!

ALIENS AND UFOS

INVESTIGATING HISTORY'S MYSTERIES

Louise Spilsbury

CHERITON
CHILDREN'S BOOKS

Published in 2024 by **Cheriton Children's Books**
1 Bank Drive West, Shrewsbury, Shropshire, SY3 9DJ, UK

© 2024 Cheriton Children's Books

First Edition

Author: Louise Spilsbury
Designer: Jessica Moon
Editor: Jennifer Sanderson
Proofreader: Katie Dicker

Picture credits: Cover: Shutterstock/3dmotus (fg), Shutterstock/Houchi (bg). Inside: p1: Shutterstock/photoBeard, p4: Shutterstock/Raggedstone, p5: Shutterstock/Fotokita, p6: Shutterstock/Merlin74, p7: Shutterstock/Akimov Konstantin, p8: Shutterstock/Phongsak Meedaenphai, p9b: Shutterstock/videobuzzing, p9t: Shutterstock/Ron Ramtang, p10: Shutterstock/Malbert, p11: Shutterstock/ImageBank4u, p12: Shutterstock/lu_sea, p13: Shutterstock/HannaTor, p14: Wikimedia Commons/Shahram Sharifi, p15: Shutterstock/Renata Barbarino, p17b: Shutterstock/Harry Zimmerman, p17t: Shutterstock/Richard Coombs, p18: Shutterstock/Marko Aliaksandr, p19: Wikimedia Commons/Paul Trent, p20: Shutterstock/Fer Gregory, p21: Shutterstock/Blueee77, p22: Shutterstock/SciePro, p23: Shutterstock/Lucian Coman, p24: Shutterstock/Fer Gregory, p25: Shutterstock/MyImages - Micha, p26: Shutterstock/Stocksnapper, p27: Shutterstock/Mervas, p27: Shutterstock/Yuriy Mazur, p28: Shutterstock/MyImages - Micha, p29: Shutterstock/MarinaP, p30: Shutterstock/Raggedstone, p31: Shutterstock/Fer Gregory, p32: Shutterstock/ImageBank4u, p33: Shutterstock/photoBeard, p35b: Shutterstock/ImageBank4u, p35t: Shutterstock/Renatas Repcinskas, p36: Shutterstock/Ed Weiner, p37: Shutterstock/Darkdiamond67, p38: Shutterstock/zhengzaishuru, p39: Wikimedia Commons/NASA/JPL, p40: Shutterstock/Dima Zel, p41: Shutterstock/Muratart, p42: Shutterstock/Dima Zel, p43: Shutterstock/Gorodenkoff, p44: Wikimedia Commons/Kevin Gill, p45: Shutterstock/Marti Bug Catcher.

Printed in China

Please visit our website,
www.cheritonchildrensbooks.com
to see more of our high-quality books.

CONTENTS

CHAPTER 1

THE TRUTH IS OUT THERE!

Are we alone in the universe? In a **cosmos** so vast, our planet is nothing more than a tiny speck of dust. Looking up from Earth into the night sky, the darkness of space is filled with the gleaming Moon, twinkling stars, the distant outlines of planets, and the promise of more worlds beyond. Sometimes, a flash of light streaks suddenly across the blackening sky, leading us to question what we have seen. Is it any wonder that since the dawn of time, people have asked what else might exist in space, and if there are other life forms, will they visit us on Earth?

Strange Sightings

There have been reports of strange objects in the sky for centuries. When there are no clear or logical explanations for these sightings, this often leads people to believe that the objects are spaceships called unidentified flying objects, or UFOs. Around the world, many people also claim to have seen or been contacted by aliens. An alien is an extraterrestrial life form, or a being from beyond Earth.

Sometimes, strange moving objects in the sky are identified as something less mysterious, such as a comet or satellite. Other times, people can find no explanation for these phenomena...

Taken, Too

Some people say that they have been taken by aliens into their UFOs and questioned about life on Earth. Others say they have even been experimented on. Some of these people believe aliens are out there somewhere, watching us—but where?

In reports of alien sightings, extraterrestrials often look a little like humans but with a larger head, huge and often snakelike eyes, and gray or green skin.

Aliens and the Ancients

How can we know if aliens exist and if they have ever visited Earth? Some people believe that the signs are easy to find. They say that ancient people did not have the ability or equipment to build structures such as the Egyptian pyramids, and that they could have done so only with help from more advanced beings. They even point to images of aliens depicted, or shown, in ancient **civilizations**. And there are many eyewitness reports of alien encounters. So, is the truth really out there?

SET TO SPOOK!

In this book, we are going to explore some of the most mystifying and unsettling reports about alien encounters—reports that have been made by ordinary people, scientists, and military personnel, or employees. Some of the stories will send shivers down your spine. Some of them will leave you truly spooked!

Aliens from Long Ago

It is hard to imagine how incredible structures such as the ancient Egyptian pyramids could have been built thousands of years ago without the help of modern machines. Could aliens have visited ancient people and helped them achieve such wonders? Do images drawn by people thousands of years ago and written descriptions from the past provide evidence, or proof, that they saw UFOs and aliens?

Evidence from the Past

Ancient Egyptians painted images and symbols called hieroglyphs onto the walls of their tombs and pyramids. **Archeologists** have found some images that can't be explained, such as a set of 3,000-year-old hieroglyphs showing flying machines and a UFO that looks like an upside-down dinner plate. Could it be these images are evidence that aliens from a distant world visited Earth long ago?

The hieroglyphs on this tomb in an ancient Egyptian temple seem to show a UFO.

Could this be a UFO?

Roman Sightings

There have been spooky sightings beyond ancient Egypt too. Greek historian Plutarch described how the Roman Army saw a strange, unexplained light in the sky as they advanced on an enemy. He wrote: "... all on a sudden, the sky burst asunder [apart], and a huge, flame-like body was seen to fall between the two armies. In shape, it was most like a wine-jar and, in color, like molten [melted] silver."

Running in Terror

Plutarch said that the strange object in the sky made the two armies stop fighting and run from the battlefield in fear. Some people argue that the Roman Army most likely saw a meteorite, which is a piece of space rock, or a comet. Perhaps we'll never truly know what the cause of the strange sight was.

Drawing Aliens?

In the Visoki Dečani **monastery** in Kosovo, Europe, there is a fourteenth-century painting showing the crucifixion of Jesus Christ. It shows unusual objects that seem to suggest aliens once visited Earth. On either side of Jesus' head there are images of what appear to be figures driving small spacecraft. While some people believe the painting shows aliens, historians suggest that it simply shows the Sun and Moon.

SPOOKED!

Was one of the Egyptian kings an alien? Ancient Egyptian hieroglyphs and statues show Pharaoh Akhenaten with a very long skull and neck, and an enlarged chest, not unlike the aliens depicted today. Some say this was likely to be the result of a genetic defect (a problem with a person's genes, or the codes that determine how they look). But is another explanation that Akhenaten was, in fact, an extraterrestrial?

ANCIENT ALIENS

Spooky Symbols

If you walk across the **remote** Nazca desert in Peru, you might not notice anything unusual in the soil. But if you fly above the land, it's a different story altogether. From above you can see the famous Nazca lines. These are a series of shapes of animals and complicated patterns carved into the land. These images cover a huge area, and they have been there for around 2,000 years. Some people believe that aliens made the lines.

Signs for the Sky

The huge shapes and images in the Nazca desert extend over an area of almost 190 square miles (492 sq km).

There are straight and clear lines that form shapes including triangles, spirals, and rectangles. There are also more than 350 images. The images include about 70 pictures of animals and plants, some of which measure up to 1,200 feet (366 m) long.

Amazing Images

The images in the desert include a spider, hummingbird, cactus, and a bird of prey called a condor. They also include a monkey, whale, llama, duck, flower, tree, lizard, and human being. The Nazca lines are so huge that the only way the images can properly be seen is from the sky—but the ancient Nazca people of Peru could not fly!

The pictures formed by the Nazca lines are clear only when viewed directly from above. At ground level, no one can clearly see the drawings.

Were the Nazca lines built to help ancient visitors from space land their ships, as some people suggest?

Extraterrestrial Etchers

Some people cannot believe that an ancient civilization such as the Nazca could have drawn the images in the desert without being able to fly. One explanation for the lines is that some Nazca people climbed nearby hills and sent instructions to people below. Those on the ground could have laid ropes to create outlines for the shapes. Then they could have used sticks to etch, or scratch, into the surface of reddish rock to reveal the lighter-colored sand beneath.

Mystery of the Lines

However, explanation for how the lines were created doesn't solve the biggest mystery: for whom were the lines created and why can they be seen only from above? Some people suggest aliens made the lines, and that some were used as runways for their spacecraft. They also suggest that the Nazca people made the images to send messages to aliens.

For the Gods?

Could the lines perhaps be meant for Nazca gods, asking for rain to help the people grow crops in the dry desert? Perhaps the "gods" that the Nazca worshiped were actually aliens! Only one thing is certain, the meaning of the incredible Nazca lines remains largely shrouded in mystery.

CHAPTER 2

MYSTERIOUS UFOS

It isn't easy to dismiss UFO sightings. Thousands of UFO sightings are reported every year and people from all backgrounds—from ordinary people to experienced pilots and government officials—have reported seeing strange objects in the sky.

Believe What You See?

Many of the UFO sightings that are investigated are revealed to have been natural occurrences. Sometimes, aircraft, bright lights, and meteors are mistaken for UFOs. Other times, human-made satellites and space junk that burns up in Earth's **atmosphere** are thought to be UFOs, too.

It is not always easy to accurately figure out how big or small something is in the sky because there are no background objects to compare them to. And when objects in the sky are seen reflected in clear glass or plastic, the light can be distorted, or changed, which makes those objects appear saucer shaped. Even so, many UFO sightings remain unaccounted for. Is this because of a lack of evidence or because the object was simply too strange to be explained?

Sometimes, unusually shaped clouds or lights in the sky can make people think that they have seen a UFO, but often they are just optical illusions.

Kenneth Arnold said he saw flying saucers weaving at high speed between the peaks of the Cascade Mountains. Other people too claim they have made similar sightings of UFOs.

Flying Saucers

A pilot named Kenneth Arnold first described UFOs as "flying saucers" in 1947. He was flying in Washington State when he saw nine strange discs flying "like a saucer skipping on water." After newspapers reported these sightings, many more people said they had also seen giant flying saucers in the sky. The public was on edge, and the military was worried that the objects could be enemy planes. After all, it had been only two years since the end of World War II (1939–1945). In 1948, the US Air Force launched Project Blue Book to investigate UFOs and to figure out if they were a threat.

From Doubt to Belief

Astronomer J. Allen Hynek led Project Blue Book. His job was to use a scientific approach to investigate UFOs and to figure out which cases were actually sightings of space objects such as planets, stars, or meteors. From 1948 to 1969, the project recorded 12,618 sightings of UFOs. Many of these were identified as **astronomical** objects and around one-third were balloons, satellites, and aircraft! Yet still, about 700 of sightings remained unexplained. Hynek spent years **debunking** UFO sightings but at the end of his career, he too had begun to believe that some of the sightings were real.

SPOOKED!

Around 40 million Americans say they have seen or know someone who has seen a UFO.

Pilots described foo fighters as red, orange, or green, and moving so quickly they often out-maneuvered the airplanes they were chasing. But could the foo fighters perhaps have been cloud formations?

Enemy Aircraft or UFOs?

On February 24, 1942, during World War II, people in Los Angeles reported seeing Japanese aircraft over the city. The US Army fired more than 1,000 bullets into the sky but they hit nothing, and no evidence of enemy aircraft was ever found. The Army was puzzled.

What Was Out There?

After the event, the Army declared the event a false alarm and stated that a **weather balloon** may have been mistaken for enemy aircraft. However, a photograph showing lights pointing toward something strange in the sky was printed in a newspaper two days later.

Some said the process of printing the picture made a smoky area in the sky appear spooky. Others believed it was proof of a UFO.

Foo Fighters

"Foo fighter" was the name given to an unexplained object that fighter pilots spotted in the air during World War II. In November 1944, for example, the crew of a Bristol Beaufighter described seeing "eight to ten bright orange lights off the left wing … flying through the air at high speed." The objects did not show up on **radar**. Some people suggested the objects were secret enemy weapons or thunderstorms creating a glow around an aircraft. Others believed they were UFOs.

Texan Terror

On the evening of August 25, 1951, in Lubbock, Texas, a group of university scientists was hanging out in a backyard when they saw around 30 very bright lights whizzing across the sky. Over the next few weeks, many other people reported strange sightings. One woman described seeing a large flying object that looked like "an airplane without a body." She said it had pairs of glowing blue-colored lights on the back edge of its wings.

Birds? No Way!

A local newspaper published the story and Project Blue Book sent Captain Edward Ruppelt to investigate. Ruppelt could not prove the photos were fakes, and he concluded that people had seen birds called plovers, not UFOs. He said the birds' undersides had reflected street light, which confused people.

The unusual thing about the Lubbock Lights episode is that UFO sightings are usually one-off events but these lights were observed many times and by hundreds of people.

Most eyewitnesses were not convinced by Ruppelt's suggestion that the UFOs were plovers, like those shown here. They said they had never seen plovers fly as fast as the lights moved!

More Unsolved Mysteries

In 1976, there were reports that Iranian fighter jets had been battling UFOs in the skies above Tehran in the Middle East. The story began on September 19, when at least four people called in sightings of a bright light in the sky. The army swiftly sent two F-4 Phantom fighter planes to investigate. This is when things took a strange turn...

Out of Control

The pilots of the fighter planes said that as they approached the object, their flight control panels began to malfunction, or stop working properly. When one pilot saw a bright light coming from the UFO, he assumed it was a missile and tried to shoot it down but his weapons control panel jammed. Without a functioning plane, he had no choice but to return to base. As he did so, he saw a glowing trail of light shoot toward the ground.

Could It Be Jupiter?

Some astronomers say that the planet Jupiter would have been especially bright in the sky that night, and the first sightings of the UFO put it where Jupiter would have been. The objects moving toward the ground could have been trails of meteors. There are also reports that the dated F-4 jet's weapons controls could have failed on that plane because it had electrical problems earlier. No one knows exactly what happened that night, and if the lights were indeed UFOs.

Did jet plane pilots mistake the planet Jupiter for a UFO or did they really see an alien spacecraft?

Waves of UFOs

Between 1989 and 1990, there was a series of reports of UFO sightings in Belgium, Europe, which became known as the "Belgian UFO wave." Many people, including three separate pairs of police officers, reported seeing strange spacecraft traveling across the skies. Military radar managed to lock onto the objects, and Belgian F-16 fighter planes were sent to investigate. The strange thing was that as soon as the jets closed in on the location of the objects, the objects disappeared from radar screens and the lights vanished too. Then, a photo of a flying object was taken and circulated around the world. Was this evidence of a UFO?

Hoaxes and Questions

After investigation, it seems the wave of sightings began with a hoax. A hoax is a trick to make something fake seem real or true. Official reports stated that people were secretly flying some type of aircraft, and then hiding it when the planes got near, to make it seem like a UFO. The following claims of UFO sightings then made other people believe they saw similar things. Twenty years later, the photographer of the flying object admitted that it was a fake, too. However, one big question remains unanswered. How did the hoaxers make the object disappear on sophisticated radar screens?

SPOOKED!

One sighting in Belgium in November 1990 was of a triangular object with three lights. It flew slowly and without sound. Russian officials dismissed the sighting as a Russian satellite breaking up but other people were not so sure...

INVESTIGATING
UFOS

Spooky Flyers

In 2020, the US government took the decision to release classified, or top-secret, information they had collected about UFOs to the public. This included three videos that appeared to capture images of meetings between military pilots and what the government preferred to call anomalous aerial vehicles, or AAVs. One of the spookiest seems to show pilots tangling with a bizarre white-colored, Tic Tac-shaped UFO.

Mysteries in the Skies

On November 14, 2004, Super Hornet fighter jets from the military ships USS *Nimitz* and USS *Princeton* were taking part in a mission in the Pacific Ocean, about 100 miles (160 km) southwest of San Diego. For several days, the *Princeton's* highly experienced radar operators had been watching more than 100 mysterious AAVs. The AAVs were flying far higher than regular planes or military jets usually fly.

Alien Alert!

At first, the operators thought there was a glitch in their machines, so they ran checks on their advanced flight technology. Then they noticed the AAVs drop at unusually high speed to lower, busier airspace, and then disappear. This put the team on high alert.

A *Princeton* officer ordered two jet pilots to stop training maneuvers and **intercept** one of the strange objects.

A Strange Encounter

When the fighter jets arrived at their destination, lead pilot Commander David Fravor saw a strange UFO that he said was "40 feet [12m] long with no wings, just hanging close to the water." Fravor described it as shaped like a Tic Tac candy, with no **rotors**. He said it moved very quickly and strangely. "This thing would go from one way to another, similar to if you threw a ping-pong ball against the wall," he stated.

Pilots on board the *Nimitz* were carrying out routine training when they encountered the AAVs. Commander Fravor said that the AAVs were faster than anything he'd ever seen in his 16 years of flying.

Scary Moves

Fravor's wingman gave an account very similar to Fravor's. She said that she felt terrified as Fravor tried to intercept the strange craft. As Fravor flew around it, he said the craft suddenly flew straight toward his plane: "All of a sudden, it kind of turns and rapidly accelerates—beyond anything I've seen—crosses my nose, and … it's gone." As the craft disappeared, other Navy jets began launching off the aircraft carrier to chase more of the AAVs being tracked by radar. A pilot from one of these planes was able to film Fravor's strange flying object using a highly sensitive **infrared** camera. Even after close investigation, no one has been able to explain what these flying objects were.

CHAPTER 3

ALIEN ARRIVALS

Just a brief Internet search for "alien arrivals" brings up a huge number of reported sightings across the world. Some of the reports of aliens landing on Earth have been exposed as elaborate fakes and hoaxes, and no one has yet proven that aliens have visited Earth. But, that doesn't stop people from believing in them.

There are so many reports of sightings that many people believe there must be a grain of truth in some.

A Meeting in the Desert

Starting in the late 1940s, a man named George Adamski from California took many photos of what he said were flying saucers. Then, in 1952, Adamski said he had met and communicated with a visitor from Venus in the Colorado Desert, using gestures and **telepathy**. He wrote several books that included claims he had been aboard a UFO with his alien friend. Adamski became famous for his stories. Experts, including J. Allen Hynek from Project Blue Book, dismissed them as fakes.

SPOOKED!

In 2022, the US National Intelligence office examined more than 500 reported UFO sightings by US troops. While around 200 were said to be objects such as drones and balloons, about 300 of the encounters remain unexplained.

UFOs Over Oregon

In 1950, farmer Paul Trent from McMinnville in Oregon, took one of the most famous photographs of a UFO. He and his wife saw a spooky flying craft hovering nearby, perhaps waiting to land. Some experts who have studied close-ups of the pictures Paul took, say it was a model suspended, or hanging, from a wire. Yet, many people are convinced that the McMinnville photos show a UFO visiting Earth. The Trents never attempted to profit from their photographs and until they died, insisted that the sighting and photos were genuine.

Siberian Spook

In April 2011, a video of an alien lying in Siberian snow became an Internet sensation. Timur Hilall and Kirill Vlasov claimed they found the body in a crashed UFO. When they were questioned, they admitted their alien was built from bread covered with chicken skin. That same year, a woman named Marta Yegorovnam claimed she had kept an alien body in her freezer for two years and taken photos of it. She said she took it from a UFO crash site. It had a huge head, bulging eyes, and a stick-like arm. We do not know if it was a fake because authorities confiscated it.

This is one of the photographs taken by Paul Trent of the strange flying craft.

Have They Landed?

Some people believe they have found circular depressions, or shallow dents, in Earth's surface that prove aliens have landed here. In 1966, an Australian farmer said he saw a UFO taking off. He found a large circular area of flattened grass in the area of lift-off. The Air Force investigated but decided the flying saucer dents were most likely caused by whirling winds, known as dust devils, or water spouts.

Curious Circles

In 1991, two men, Doug Bower and David Chorley, admitted that they had made 200 of the crop circles that had sprung up overnight in the United Kingdom (UK) since the 1980s. The men said that they had created the unusual circles, shapes, and other patterns by flattening areas of farm cereals. Since then, crop circles have been reported worldwide in many different types of crops, leading many people to believe that some could be the work of aliens.

SPOOKED!

Across the dry **grasslands** of Namibia, Africa, there are numerous very large circular areas where no plants ever grow. These are known as fairy circles, and some measure up to 50 feet (15 m) wide. Some say they are created by insects called termites or by the harsh, dry climate. But others suspect alien activity.

Could strange circle marks in the land, like those shown below, be UFO landing sites?

Crash Landings?

Some people believe circular depressions in the ground called craters are further evidence of alien landings. Most are proven to have been caused by meteors, asteroids, and comets that crashed into Earth's surface. There are around 180 such craters worldwide, and one-third are found in North America. But were they all caused by impacts?

Was the Richat Structure created by a meteoric impact, by the unusual erosion, or wearing away, of layers of rocks over millions of years, or, as some believe, by an alien landing?

An Eye in the Desert

When **orbiting** Earth, astronauts have been fascinated by the Richat Structure, which is also known as The Eye of the Sahara. When viewed from space, this 28-mile (45 km) wide, swirling feature in the Sahara looks like a staring eye. While there are **geological** explanations for the feature, some say the series of **concentric circles** look exactlylike UFO landing pads.

Mysterious Marks

On January 8, 1981, Renato Nicolaï saw a saucer-shaped UFO land on his land in France. The gray spacecraft then lifted off from the ground and flew toward some trees. The case is interesting because the machine appeared to leave marks on the land. French authorities analyzed the marks but were unable to find any explanation for the incident.

INVESTIGATING
ALIEN ARRIVALS

Spooked in Africa

In 2022, a new documentary called *Ariel Phenomenon* was made. The film explored whether a UFO had landed near a school in Zimbabwe, Africa, in September 1994, as many witnesses claimed. What really happened outside the school? Did the schoolchildren carry out an elaborate hoax? Were the sightings a case of mass hysteria or did the children mistake a landing helicopter for a flying saucer? Perhaps the students actually witnessed an alien arrival…

Strange Saucers

September 16, 1994, had been an otherwise uneventful day at the Ariel School in Ruwa, Zimbabwe. At break time, 62 students were sent out to play while their teachers met indoors. Some of the children claim that they suddenly spotted a silvery, saucer-shaped flying object land just beyond their playground.

Haunting Humanoids

When they ran to the edge of the school grounds to get a closer look, some of the children said they saw **humanoids** emerging from the object. "It looked like it was glinting in the trees. It looked like a disc. Like a round disc," said one child. "And a person in black," said another, "with large and elongated eyes and a slit for a mouth."

The Evidence

Cynthia Hind, a UFO researcher visited the school to investigate. She asked the children to draw what they had seen. They all drew similar pictures of silvery UFOs, sometimes with alien figures nearby. A Harvard professor named John Mack then interviewed the children. He believed them too. A photographer took a photo of wedge-shaped marks and oval imprints in the school field, which many believe the UFO made.

Could It Be Real?

Those who don't believe the children point to several reasons why the story is not true. They say recent radio reports of UFO sightings, which were actually a meteor shower or satellite burning up in Earth's atmosphere, had influenced the children. They said that Mack wanted to believe the children, and prompted their stories. Perhaps one child thought they saw something and the others wanted to join in. Yet, the children are now adults and have all stuck to their stories. Mack still believes that the event may turn out to be real in some way that we do not yet understand.

Cynthia Hind suggested that as the children lived in the countryside and didn't go to the movies, they would not have seen alien images before, so this made their story more believable.

CHAPTER 4

ALIEN ABDUCTIONS

It starts when you wake at night to a strange buzzing sound, flashing lights, and tingling sensations in your body. Unable to move anything but your eyes, and unable to call out, all you can do is watch as a figure that is not human stands by your bed or approaches you! This is how some people who claim to have been abducted, or taken, by aliens describe their experience. Every year, there are many reports of people who say they were kidnapped by extraterrestrials.

Taken by Aliens

Since the 1960s, people have not only reported sightings of UFOs and landings but they have also claimed to have been kidnapped by aliens. In these reports, people sometimes say that the aliens merely visited their homes at night while they were sleeping. But in other events, the aliens took the people away, sometimes through the walls of their houses! They beamed victims up into their UFOs using a mysterious, possibly **electromagnetic**, force.

Reports of close encounters with aliens and alien abductions have continued for decades.

Murder or Abduction?

On November 5, 1975, seven men finished a hard day's work thinning trees in the Apache-Sitgreaves National Forests, Arizona, and headed home. On the way, they suddenly spotted a "luminous object, shaped like a flattened disk" hovering over some felled trees. Travis Walton got out of the truck to investigate. The rest watched in horror, as a bright blue light zapped Walton and tossed his body into the air. The men fled the scene in terror and reported it to the police. For the five days Walton was missing, his coworkers were suspected of murdering him. When Travis reappeared, he said he had memories of aliens standing over him.

Campground Terror

In 1977, Terry Lovelace and his friend Toby were sitting around a campfire in Devil's Den State Park, Arkansas, when suddenly, everything went quiet. A black triangular object as wide as two city blocks with three bright lights appeared overhead. A blue laser beam hovered over the men, and they became sleepy. When Lovelace woke up, Toby was looking out of the tent at 12 figures and the UFO. Toby told Lovelace aliens took and hurt them both. Lovelace says that since then **hypnosis** has brought back more memories of being inside the UFO and encountering creatures inside it.

SPOOKED!

Some people say that when taken aboard a spacecraft, the aliens questioned or examined them. They also claim that medical experiments and tests were carried out on them. Others say the aliens gave them important information about the future of Earth.

Police Sighting

Police officer Alan Godfrey encountered a large, mysterious diamond-shaped object hovering close to the ground in Yorkshire, UK, as he neared the end of his shift at 5 a.m. on November 28, 1980. Godfrey sketched the UFO on his police notepad but was then blinded by a bright light. The next thing he knew, he woke up 30 minutes later and the UFO was nowhere to be seen.

Sticking to His Story

Godfrey had no idea what had happened during that lost time but his left boot was ripped and he had an itchy red mark, like a burn, on his foot. He believed aliens had abducted him. Godfrey was teased for years but when interviewed again in 2021, he still said his story was true. He said, "I know what I saw that night was real, nuts and bolts. If I'd got out and thrown a brick at it, it would have gone, 'Clang!'"

People who have encountered aliens are convinced what they saw was real.

SPOOKED!

Identical twins Audrey and Debbie Hewins from Maine claim that from the age of four they were visited by small humanoids with large, bald heads, gray skin, and big black eyes. Each visit was accompanied by a buzzing sound, a blinding blue light, and glowing fog. From the age of 12, they said the aliens often took them aboard their spaceship, too. In 2006, as adults, the twins set up a support group called Starborn to help other people cope with the distress an alien encounter can cause.

Official Belief

British Ministry of Defence (MOD) investigator Nick Pope researched Godfrey's case. He believes that Godfrey is genuine, stating, "He had a lot to potentially lose by coming out with this and yet stuck to his guns." It seems that this case of alien abduction left a lot of people stumped.

New York Nightmare

At 3 a.m. on November 30, 1989, a reddish-orange UFO was reported hovering over the Brooklyn Bridge in New York City. Several eyewitnesses also reported seeing a woman named Linda Cortile floating out from the window of her 12th-floor apartment, directly below the UFO. Three aliens were abducting her!

Like a Movie!

One witness said she thought, "Somebody must be making a movie. This must be a movie, because this is impossible." Another witness said the UFO was enormous. There were no connections between the witnesses, two of whom were police officers. Cortile returned to her building later that night unharmed, with little memory of her missing hours.

At least one witness said their car stopped suddenly on Brooklyn Bridge when the UFO appeared.

Theories about Abductions

There are so many reports from people who have had alien encounters or been abducted by aliens—what possible explanation could there be for them other than that they are true? Most of the people involved are discovered to have no mental illness, apart from the effects of the **trauma**. They are often smart, professional people who have no history of telling lies or making up stories. Many of the people who recount, or tell others about, these events truly believe they are real, and some suffer from severe distress afterward.

Paralyzed by Sleep

Some alien abduction reports are put down to a condition called sleep paralysis. Sleep paralysis can happen when people are waking up or on the edge of falling asleep, for example, when tired and driving late at night. In that moment, people feel aware but can't move or speak.

Strange Sensations

People experiencing sleep paralysis often feel like a heavy weight is pressing on their chest or that they are floating or flying. In some cases, people get other **symptoms**, such as a very strong feeling that something or someone is in the room with them. Sleep paralysis usually only lasts for a minute or two but sufferers say it can feel like it lasts for many hours.

Sleep paralysis often makes people feel like they are floating or flying. Could this explain why some people feel they were beamed up into UFOs?

Experiencing Horror

Many psychiatrists who study reports of alien abductions think that the people involved had hallucinations. Hallucinations are **sensory** experiences that appear real but are created by the mind. They can affect all five of the senses. For example, a person might hear a voice that no one else in the room can hear or see things that are not real. Hallucinations can be very scary. When someone is hallucinating, they may see strange lights moving around them or spooky figures lurking nearby. It is also common for people to have hallucinations during sleep paralysis.

Wanting to Believe in Aliens

Some psychiatrists suggest that people see UFOs and aliens because they want to believe there are other forms of life in the universe. Experts say that many people have a need to feel their lives are meaningful, and a belief in aliens may suggest that a greater, more powerful intelligence exists.

Could believing they have been abducted by aliens give some people a sense of importance?

SPOOKED!

Some people who feel they have had alien encounters want the events to be true because that would mean they are special in some way. Most abductions leave no evidence. However, the people involved say the real evidence for the abductions is the similarities in the stories themselves, and that people believe they actually happened.

ALIEN ABDUCTIONS

Spooky Kidnapping

Late one dark night in September 1961, Betty and Barney Hill were traveling home to Portsmouth, New Hampshire after a vacation in Canada. At some point during their drive, they realized that they were being followed down the empty, winding roads by a white glowing object that was spinning in the air.

Hunted by Humanoids

After a while, the couple stopped their car near North Woodstock. Barney got out. Through his binoculars, he watched a UFO tilt downward and start dropping toward land. He later said he was able to make out strange humanoids wearing shiny black uniforms. They were looking at the couple from the spacecraft's brightly lit windows. Struck by fear, Barney jumped back into the car.

Spooky Sensations

Suddenly, the Hills became aware they were in their car but a lot farther along the road than they had been when they saw the UFO. When they arrived home, they realized their journey had taken a couple of hours longer than it should have taken. They also had a feeling that something unusual had happened to them. Their watches had stopped working and Betty spotted unexplained stains on her dress. There were also some marks on the underside of their car.

Sinister Side Effects

After the event, Betty began to have nightmares about spooky faces and medical examinations. Barney started to feel uneasy and unwell. These prompted the couple to make an appointment with Dr. Benjamin Simon, a Boston psychiatrist. He started to treat the couple with hypnosis therapy for what he thought was anxiety, or feeling nervous. However, while under hypnosis, the Hills both told the doctor they were abducted by strange figures and taken aboard a flying saucer.

Were the Hills followed by an alien spacecraft?

Both Betty and Barney Hill say they remember being inside a UFO.

Strange Experiments

Under hypnosis, the couple recalled being examined for up to two hours. Barney spoke of lying on a table that was too short, and the aliens taking out his false teeth. Betty remembered them taking skin scrapings and nail clippings. The Hills said that after the abduction, the aliens had erased their memories of the experience.

What Is the Truth?

Could the Hills be telling the truth? They did not try to make money from their experience. They only talked about it after the story was discovered and published by a newspaper in 1965. Psychiatrists think that because the Hills were tired and driving late, they may have experienced sleep paralysis and had hallucinations. The sense of floating during hallucinations may have made them believe aliens abducted them. We'll never know for certain what happened that night…

CHAPTER 5

ALIEN INVESTIGATIONS

If extraterrestrials do not exist, why are there so many reports of UFOs and alien investigations, and why are there so many ongoing cases today? One of the most famous of all investigations is the Roswell mystery.

Reports from Roswell

During the 1940s, the US Air Force was carrying out top-secret tests at a base near Roswell, New Mexico. It was sending **surveillance balloons** carrying microphones into the sky to listen out for Russian **atomic bomb** tests.

UFO Disaster?

The base's activities had already intrigued nearby people. In July 1947, William Brazel found some **debris** on the ranch where he worked. Brazel thought it was from a UFO crash. The military swiftly cleared the debris away, and seemed to confirm Brazel's suspicions by saying that a "flying disc" had crashed near Roswell.

Changing Their Story

Soon afterward, military officials were keen to play down the incident. They said it was a **weather balloon** and showed reporters pieces of metal, rubber, and wood they said came from the crash site. One theory is that the US Air Force was lying because it didn't want to admit it was using surveillance balloons.

Some people think the US military was covering up the fact that a UFO had crashed in the area.

This is a model of the Roswell alien.

Autopsy on an Alien

Perhaps the Roswell mystery would have been forgotten but 40 years later, it made headlines again. In 1989, Glenn Dennis, a **mortuary** worker at the Roswell base in 1947, claimed that he knew a nurse who had accidentally stumbled into a room where doctors were examining three aliens.

Words of Witnesses

Dennis said the nurse described the creatures as having small bodies, long thin arms, and big, bald heads. When his story broke, other people said they too had seen UFOs and aliens near Roswell. Officials said Dennis's story was false but that doesn't explain the other witness reports.

SPOOKED!

The Roswell story took another unusual turn in May 1995, when a movie of the 1947 alien autopsy aired on Fox TV. In it, surgeons are seen cutting into the body of one of the aliens that allegedly died in the UFO crash at Roswell. The movie convinced some people. Most dismissed it as a fake. Close-ups on the alien body were blurry, and it appeared to be made of rubber. In the end, British video producer, Ray Santilli, admitted he had made the film, and that it was a hoax.

ALIEN CASES

Spooky Cover-Ups

In 2022, a documentary titled "Moment of Contact" was released. It centered on a series of events in January 1996, when locals in Varginha, Brazil, reported seeing one or more strange creatures and a UFO crash. They claim officials took the dead aliens away for investigation.

Crash Landing

In the documentary, college professor Carlos de Souza describes seeing a submarine-shaped spacecraft the size of a school bus, with smoke coming out of a rip in its rear. He claimed the UFO jerked around in the sky and then fell to the ground. De Souza says he found pieces of foil-like metal at the crash site, which returned to their original shape when he tried to crumple them in his hand. He claims military soldiers then appeared, and chased him away.

Strange Creatures

Seven days later, three young girls spotted a tiny, frightened creature crouching by a wall between two houses. A description noted: "It had red eyes, oily skin. I couldn't see an open mouth. Not smiling… Sad expression. Shrunken back. It didn't have hair. Eyes three times bigger than ours." When the girls later returned to the site, all that was left was a print in the dirt. It seemed to have been made by a foot with three very long toes.

A Military Cover-Up?

The documentary suggests that the Brazilian police and military set up a **blockade** in a local neighborhood and captured the two creatures. At this point, one of the beings is said to have scratched an officer, Marco Chereze. Chereze became sick and told a doctor what had happened, before dying of an infection.

Death Threats

Vitório Pacaccini, a UFO investigator, reported that in 2012, a senior officer showed him a film of a "skinny, weak, and fragile," creature with "a big head with red eyes and no pupils … and three **protuberances** on the top of its head." Pacaccini claims to have videotaped interviews with at least seven officers about the encounter. He says he keeps the tape hidden because, since accusing the military of a cover-up, he's received death threats.

Paralyzing Photographs

UFO researcher Patricia Fernandes Silva also claims that the former sheriff of Varginha showed her a color photo of two creatures, one with "three high **abscesses** on the forehead." She says the former sheriff told her that his hands had been paralyzed ever since touching one of the creatures.

"Moment of Contact" ends with the suggestion that the crashed UFO from Varginha was loaded onto a US Air Force plane in Brazil and taken back to the United States.

Evidence of Investigations

Over the years, governments around the world have taken an interest in UFOs and have released documents and reports to the public in order to share their findings. The United States, Russia, France, and the UK have all released reports on UFOs. Back in 1999, a journalist named Leslie Kean leaked a French file on UFOs, showing both generals and admirals believed the unexplained phenomena could potentially be extraterrestrial.

Spooky Step Ups

A US Navy task force reviewed 144 sightings by US government personnel that occurred between 2004 and 2021. The sightings remain "unidentified." These reports do not use the term "UFO." Instead they use the name unidentified aerial phenomenon, or UAP, and Deputy Defense Secretary David Norquist created the Unidentified Aerial Phenomena Task Force on August 14, 2020. Does this name change suggest that the US government is now taking the mysterious sightings seriously?

In 2023, three UFOs of vastly different shapes and sizes were shot down by US authorities in less than two weeks.

SPOOKED!

In February 2023, the US military opened fire on flying objects in North America. The government says that China sent at least one of the four objects to spy on the United States. China claimed the one object was a weather balloon that drifted off course. The other three were unexplained.

Avi Loeb suggested that Oumuamua, a torpedo-shaped object from beyond our Solar System spotted in 2017, was an alien spaceship.

Spying on Earth

In July 2022, the US Department of Defense (DOD) established the Pentagon's All-domain Anomaly Resolution Office (AARO) to detect and investigate UFOs, particularly in areas where they potentially affect military activities. Sean M. Kirkpatrick, director of the AARO, and Avi Loeb, an astronomer at Harvard University, both called for a far more thorough approach to evaluating UAP sightings.

Hovering Over Us

The team found that a number of UAP sightings could be explained by optical illusions or the limitations of equipment. However, the team also says it is possible an extraterrestrial spaceship could be hovering around our Solar System, sending out tiny **probes** to gather and send back information about Earth and other planets. These probes would likely be too small for telescopes to detect.

CHAPTER 6

SEARCHING IN SPACE

Why wait for aliens and UFOs to find us? All around the world people are discovering new ways to explore space and look for evidence of extraterrestrial life. A range of amazing technologies is used on Earth and sent into space to search for alien life.

High-Tech Search

The technologies being used to explore space have already shown us that the planet Mars may once have had the ingredients necessary for life. They also show that some of the moons orbiting other planets in and beyond our Solar System have icy oceans with liquid water beneath. They could be home to some types of alien life forms.

Signals from Space

Radio telescopes on Earth are able to pick up signals and other signs of activity by aliens in space.

In 2022, astronomers across Canada and the United States detected a strange and repeated radio signal from a far-off **galaxy**. It flashed in an unusually regular pattern. Astronomers think the signal may have been caused when the **cores** of giant stars collapsed. Or could something else be responsible for the signal? Daniele Michili, a researcher at the Massachusetts Institute of Technology (MIT) described its repeated boom, boom, boom pattern as "like a heartbeat."

Large radio telescopes are able to pick up brief signals, such as the flash of a distant powerful laser.

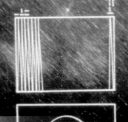

Voyagers 1 and 2 carry identical copper discs that can tell the story of Earth if found by aliens in deep space.

Probing Space

Probes are launched into space on powerful rockets. Once in space, a probe separates from its rocket and follows a set course programmed into it, far out into our Solar System. Probes carry special cameras, telescopes, and other instruments to gather information that they send back to Earth by radio signal.

Into Outer Space

Voyager 1 and 2 are NASA probes that were launched in 1977, and are still traveling through space. They were designed to gather information about the planets Jupiter and Saturn but since doing that, they are now exploring regions of space where no other object from Earth has gone before. In 2013, Voyager 1 sent a sound recording back to Earth as it left our Solar System. It was the first-ever recording of sounds in **interstellar** space.

SPOOKED!

Inside each of the Voyager probes is a gold-plated copper disc, along with a cartridge, needle, and instructions shown as symbols that explain how to play the disc. The disc contains pictures, sounds, and words in different languages. If aliens find the probes, they could play the discs to find out about Earth and its people.

Is There Life on Mars?

The idea of Martians living on the planet Mars, has intrigued people for decades. Before space exploration took off, Mars was thought to be the most likely planet in our Solar System on which extraterrestrials might live.

Searching for Evidence

Since 1976, NASA has sent five rovers and five landers to Mars. In 2016, the six-wheeled Curiosity rover took **samples** from the Gale Crater that contained carbon, something that would be a sign of life on Earth. The rover also recorded surges of methane, a gas that is produced by natural processes on Earth. It also discovered rounded pebbles, which show water once flowed on Mars.

Lakes and Life

Perseverance—nicknamed Percy—is a car-sized Mars rover that began to explore the surface of Mars in February 2021. It searched for signs of past and present life in the Jezero Crater, which astronomers believe was once an ancient lake. On Earth, every living thing we know of needs water to survive, so finding evidence of plenty of water in the past gives the rover its best chance of finding evidence of life on Mars.

This artist's illustration shows the Perseverance rover. A hovering rocket-powered spacecraft called a skycrane gently lowered the rover onto the surface of Mars.

Alien Life on Other Moons

Many astronomers think that exploring icy moons in the outer Solar System will be our next best chance of finding alien life forms. The moons include Saturn's Enceladus and Jupiter's Europa. The Cassini-Huygens space probe mission that explored Saturn from 2000 to 2019 found signs of **hydrothermal vents** on the ocean floor of Enceladus. On Earth, **bacteria** obtain the energy they need to live from these vents, which release heat and chemicals from the core of our planet. Could this be the case on Enceladus too?

Ocean Living

Evidence suggests there is a salty ocean below Europa's thick, icy crust that could be miles deep. The water could contain the right mix of chemicals to support life, and could even be home to some form of living things. These living things are most likely to be bacteria, but could there be bigger alien animals in the water too, which feed on the bacteria?

In the future, space submarines may be able to explore the mysterious underwater worlds of other moons, such as Saturn's Enceladus.

SPOOKED!

Europa Clipper, a spacecraft designed to orbit Jupiter carrying scientific instruments, is scheduled to take off in 2024. Scientists and inventors are currently designing submarines that should be able to dive deep and explore the ocean on Jupiter's Europa. The submarines are jellyfish-like robots with semi-transparent, barrel-shaped bodies.

Exploring Exoplanets

Our Solar System is not the only place in the universe where planets are found. Scientists have discovered thousands of exoplanets. These are planets that orbit stars other than our Sun and are therefore beyond our Solar System. Thirty-four of these exoplanets are found in what is known as the "habitable zone" of their stars. This is an area not too close nor too far from their stars, where the temperature is right for liquid water to exist. If it were too hot, the water would evaporate. If it were too cold, it would freeze.

Searching Far Away

Many of the exoplanets we know about were discovered by NASA's Kepler space telescope. Space telescopes use large mirrors to collect and focus light from distant stars and take images of faraway objects. The telescopes can send and receive information from scientists on Earth. The Hubble space telescope was launched into low Earth orbit in 1990 and is still hard at work. While other space telescopes find exoplanets, Hubble was the first telescope to directly detect an exoplanet's atmosphere and then study its makeup.

If liquid water is where life on our planet started, could there be life on one or more of the exoplanets beyond our Solar System too?

> Could HabEx be the key to finding signs of alien life in the universe? And, if so, perhaps one day we will even journey to that planet.

Looking for Homes

In 2035, NASA plans to launch the Habitable Exoplanet Observatory, or HabEx, into space. It will orbit thousands of miles beyond Earth. HabEx will have a space telescope with a 13-feet- (4 m) wide mirror. It will have a huge star shield to block light from a bright star, so the telescope can image and survey its exoplanets. Its mission is to take images of exoplanets and study the chemicals in their atmospheres.

So, Is There Life Out There?

It's true that we don't have **conclusive** evidence yet that there are other planets or moons in space where alien life forms live. Yet, many people, including some scientists and astronomers, believe the signs are already there. Every year we build more advanced forms of technology that help us explore new areas of space where aliens and UFOs might be lurking. Could it be that one day soon we will find evidence of alien beings? Perhaps then some of the spooky stories about UFOs and aliens from the past may be proven true.

SPOOKED!

HabEx will carry instruments that can detect water and gases such as oxygen and carbon dioxide, which indicate signs of life.

DEEP SPACE

Spooky Life

The James Webb Space Telescope (JWST) is the largest, most powerful space telescope ever built. It was launched on December 25, 2021, and began its observations in 2022. It is able to see through the atmospheres of gas giant planets and will help us learn more about a handful of exoplanets that are similar to Earth.

Amazing Mirrors

The bigger the mirror, the more details a space telescope can see. JWST's main mirror measures more than 21 feet (6.5 m) across. In order to launch such a big mirror into space, the JWST mirror is made from 18 hexagonal panels coated in gold. The panels were folded inside a rocket for launch. They unfolded to form one large mirror when the JWST reached orbit. The panels can move and bend the mirror by amounts far smaller than the width of a human hair. They focus light precisely and concentrate it onto a secondary mirror that bounces the light to JWST's **sensors**.

Searching for Signs

The JWST mirrors are covered in a thin layer of gold to help them reflect infrared light. Infrared is a type of light that people cannot see but they feel it as heat. The JWST will use its infrared cameras to see through dust clouds in space and figure out which exoplanets have surfaces that are warm enough for life. It will also be able to detect gases such as carbon dioxide, oxygen, and methane in an exoplanet's atmosphere. Living things can release the gases, and so show life exists.

The JWST is as tall as a three-story building and as long as a tennis court. It was named after James Webb, the head of NASA during the Apollo mission that put the first human on the Moon.

Perfect Planets

The JWST is exploring the atmospheres of exoplanets for signs of life. Its first mission was to look at the TRAPPIST-1 system, an incredible collection of seven rocky exoplanets. In March 2023, the JWST measured the temperature of TRAPPIST-1b, based on the heat energy it gave off in the form of infrared light.

Only the Beginning

The result of investigation into TRAPPIST-1 b showed that the exoplanet is too hot for life and has no significant atmosphere. It seems that Trappist-1b is unlikely to have the conditions needed for life, but the mission has only just begun. Could the atmospheres of other exoplanets hold the building blocks for life or even alien life forms? We will find out soon!

Many people believe that exoplanets in the habitable zone that the JWST is looking at hold our best chance of finding alien life in the near future.

GLOSSARY

abscesses pus-filled lumps

archeologists people who study history through evidence left behind by people who lived long ago

astronomical related to the study of space

atmosphere layers of gases that surround a planet or a moon

atomic bomb a very powerful bomb

bacteria very tiny living things

blockade cutting off of an area to stop people entering or leaving it

civilizations settled and organized groups of people with government, laws, and a system of writing

comet a ball of frozen gases, rock, and dust that orbits the Sun

concentric circles circles of different sizes that have the same center point

conclusive proves something is true

cores hot, dense areas in the center of planets and stars

cosmos another word for universe

debris broken pieces or remains of something

debunking showing that something is false

electromagnetic magnetic due to a flow of electricity

galaxy a group of millions of stars, dust, and gas

geological related to the study of rocks

grasslands open, grass-filled areas

humanoids human-like beings

hydrothermal vents openings in the sea floor

hypnosis a sleep-like state in which thoughts can be influenced by someone else

infrared describes rays of light that cannot be seen but give off heat

intercept to stop something from reaching its target

interstellar between the stars

monastery a building in which monks live

mortuary a place where a dead body is prepared for a funeral

optical illusions things that you think you see, but are not there

phenomena strange or unusual things that often can't be explained

probes spacecraft that travel through space to collect information

protuberances lumps that stick out from a surface

radar a system that uses radio waves to detect aircraft and other objects

remote far away

rotors machine parts that spin

samples small amounts of something

satellite an electronic device placed in orbit around Earth

sensors devices that are used to spy on people and places

sensory linked to the senses

surveillance balloons devices that spy on people and places

symptoms signs of disease or illness

telepathy mind-reading

trauma a scary or disturbing event or experience

weather balloon a device used to study conditions in the atmosphere

FIND OUT MORE

Books

Bolte, Mari. *Visitors from Outer Space* (Aliens Among Us: The Evidence). Cherry Lake Publishing, 2022.

Hubbard, Ben. *What Do We Know About the Roswell Incident?* Penguin Workshop, 2023.

Mayer, Kirsten. *What Do We Know About Alien Abduction?* Penguin Workshop, 2023.

Peterson, Megan Cooley. *Searching for Aliens with Tech* (Paranormal Tech). Capstone Press, 2023.

Websites

Discover more alien and UFO stories at:
www.history.com/ufo-stories

For NASA's take on the subject of UFOs see:
www.nasa.gov/feature/faq-unidentified-aerial-phenomena-uapsufos

Find out more about aliens and UFOs at:
https://science.howstuffworks.com/space/aliens-ufos

For the latest news about aliens and UFOs visit:
www.space.com/topics/ufos-extraterrestrials

Publisher's note to educators and parents:
All the websites featured above have been carefully reviewed to ensure that they are suitable for students. However, many websites change often, and we cannot guarantee that a site's future contents will continue to meet our high standards of educational value. Please be advised that students should be closely monitored whenever they access the Internet.

INDEX

About the Author

Louise Spilsbury is an award-winning children's book author. She has written countless books about history and science. In writing and researching this book, she is more spooked than ever by the idea that aliens and UFOs may be out there!